THE OFFICIAL
CELTIC
ANNUAL 2020

Written by Joe Sullivan
Designed by Chris Dalrymple

g

A Grange Publication

© 2019. Published by Grange Communications Ltd., Edinburgh, under licence from Celtic Football Club. Printed in the EU.

Photographs by Alan Whyte and Ryan Whyte, Angus Johnston, Celtic Multi-Media.

ISBN 978-1-913034-15-3

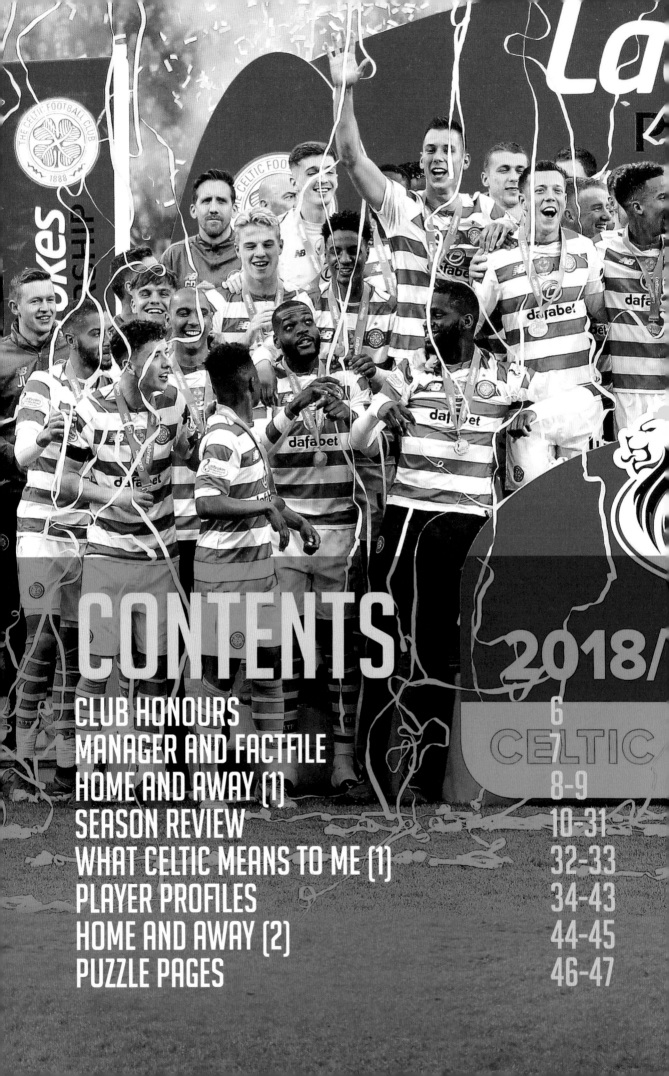

CONTENTS

2018/

CELTIC

CLUB HONOURS

SCOTTISH LEAGUE WINNERS [50 TIMES]

1892/93, 1893/94, 1895/96, 1897/98,
1904/05, 1905/06, 1906/07, 1907/08,
1908/09, 1909/10, 1913/14, 1914/15,
1915/16, 1916/17, 1918/19, 1921/22,
1925/26, 1935/36, 1937/38, 1953/54,

1965/66, 1966/67, 1967/68, 1968/69,
1969/70, 1970/71, 1971/72, 1972/73,
1973/74, 1976/77, 1978/79, 1980/81,
1981/82, 1985/86, 1987/88, 1997/98,
2000/01, 2001/02, 2003/04, 2005/06,

2006/07, 2007/08, 2011/12, 2012/13,
2013/14, 2014/15, 2015/16, 2016/17,
2017/18, 2018/19

SCOTTISH CUP WINNERS [39 TIMES]

1892, 1899, 1900, 1904, 1907, 1908,
1911, 1912, 1914, 1923, 1925, 1927,
1931, 1933, 1937, 1951, 1954, 1965,
1967, 1969, 1971, 1972, 1974, 1975,
1977, 1980, 1985, 1988, 1989, 1995,
2001, 2004, 2005, 2007, 2011, 2013,
2017, 2018, 2019

LEAGUE CUP WINNERS [18 TIMES]

1956/57, 1957/58, 1965/66, 1966/67,
1967/68, 1968/69, 1969/70, 1974/75,
1982/83, 1997/98, 1999/00, 2000/01,
2005/06, 2008/09, 2014/15, 2016/17,
2017/18, 2018/19

EUROPEAN CUP WINNERS 1967
CORONATION CUP WINNERS 1953

NEIL LENNON

MANAGER FACTFILE

D.O.B:
25/06/71

Born:
Lurgan, Ireland

Playing career record:
Manchester City (1988-90), Crewe Alexandra (1990-96), Leicester City (1996-2000), Celtic (2000-07), Nottingham Forest (2007-08), Wycombe Wanderers (2008)

Playing honours:
Leicester City: League Cup Winners: (1996/97, 1999/2000)

Celtic: Scottish Premier League Champions: (2000/01, 2001/02, 2003/04, 2005/06, 2006/07)

Scottish Cup Winners: (2000/01, 2003/04, 2004/05, 2006/07)

Scottish League Cup Winners: (2000/01, 2005/06)

UEFA Cup Runners-up: (2002/03)

As Manager:
Celtic: Scottish Premier League Champions: (2011/12, 2012/13, 2013/14, 2018/19)

Scottish Cup Winners: (2010/11, 2012/13, 2018/19)

Hibernian: Scottish Championship Winners: (2016/17)

NEIL Lennon has become rather adept at writing himself into the managerial history of Celtic Football Club. First of all, not only was he the first interim manager to be offered the job permanently, he has now achieved that feat twice after taking over from fellow Irishman, Brendan Rodgers in March, 2019.

Also, in season 2012/13, he became only the third Celt to achieve the domestic double of league and Scottish Cup as both a player and manager - joining club giants, Jock Stein and Billy McNeill.

He is now following in their footsteps again, and arrived last year to lead the team once more to that double, which, of course, were the final two trophies of a truly astounding Treble Treble, with the title win also sealing the eight-in-a-row that he himself started earlier in the decade.

The Irishman was, of course, used to parading silverware around Paradise as a Celtic player, with five titles, four Scottish Cups and two League Cups won after being brought to the club by Martin O'Neill and, when he took over as manager in 2010, the silver kept on flowing.

Another three titles (all in a row) and two Scottish Cups were won while Neil Lennon held the reins at Celtic Park before he departed for pastures new in 2014 – but, crucially, the foundations had been set for the current eight-in-a-row and all the success that comes with that.

Bolton Wanderers and Hibernian were his next ports of call before, once more, just as in March 2010, in March 2019, Neil Lennon answered the call and he returned to Celtic to steady a ship that could have veered off course. This time though, there were definite trophy targets within Celtic's sights, and he didn't let the club down when it came to delivering them.

Previously, he has followed in the footsteps of Jock Stein and Billy McNeill, now he is following in the footsteps of Neil Lennon - and he already knows how to deliver silverware to Paradise.

HOME AND AWAY...
PART ONE

HOME is where the heart is, and we all know what Paradise means to us as Celtic's home ground. What about the players' home towns, though – or their favourite holiday destinations?

We spoke to a few of the players to find out where they were brought up and where they go to during the close season.

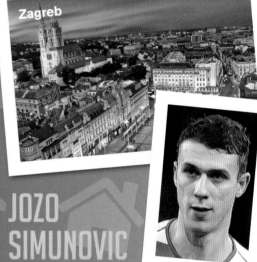
Zagreb

CRAIG GORDON

Home
A village called Balerno. It's about seven or eight miles outside Edinburgh, not far from Livingston. It's not a big village. It was a nice little village which had football parks at either end of the street and we would use trees as goalposts.

Away
Recently I was in Santorini, which was nice to see. It's a Greek Island with spectacular sunsets. I was also in Rome and Venice over the past couple of years.

JOZO SIMUNOVIC

Home
My hometown is Zagreb which is the capital city of Croatia. I was born there and I love everything about it. It's for sure my favourite place. We have proper winters with lots of snow and hot summers, it's a beautiful city all year round.

Away
There are lots of places in Croatia which I like to visit on my holidays. There are so many great places along the coast, so I couldn't say for sure which is my favourite but anywhere along the coast in Croatia is beautiful.

BALERNO

Santorini

Croatia

RYAN CHRISTIE

Home

I grew up in Inverness. When people visit it, they say it's lovely and amazing, but growing up there, it's quiet and there isn't much to do, which was probably good at the time as there was nothing else to do but play football and that probably helped me. I was there until I moved to Celtic and came down to live in the big smoke, which was a bit of a change! I don't really visit much which sounds really bad, but most of the time my family will come down and visit me in Glasgow and escape Inverness for a few days. It sounds like I'm hammering it as it's a nice city, but I just wouldn't want to stay there too long.

Away

Normally a city around Europe, I quite like a wee city break. I changed it up recently and went to Dubai and furthered my horizons, but normally I keep it very European. I liked Barcelona and Copenhagen but I'm hoping to add to that list. I would like to go somewhere in Sweden next, so maybe somewhere like Stockholm.

Inverness

Stockholm

New York

MIKEY JOHNSTON

Home

I grew up in Stepps, there's nothing special about it. I've lived there my whole life and always been in the same house. The good thing is it's close to the Academy and training at Lennoxtown as I'm only about five or 10 minutes away from Celtic Park and about 20 minutes away from Lennoxtown, so that's pretty easy. I went to St Joseph's School in Stepps when I was in primary.

Away

Recently I went to Cyprus with my pals. I also went to Dubai with the first team and I liked that, it was surreal and it was different. I like America and I might go there next as I've been there a few times and it's great. I've been to Florida but I'd like to try out New York or maybe California. The USA would be my favourite for my next holiday.

SEASON

JULY

CELTIC started preparations for their Treble Treble bid in earnest just weeks after completing the **Double Treble** when, after a week at Lennoxtown, the side headed out to Austria for their summer training camp and friendlies against **Bohemians Prague, SK Vorwarts Steyr and Sparta Prague** at the end of June and into July.

From there it was over to Dublin where a 7-0 win over Shamrock Rovers set the Celts up nicely for their first competitive game of the term and a long trip to Alashkert in Armenia where the ball was set rolling in the 45th minute as Odsonne Edouard scored the Hoops' first goal of the season.

JULY FIXTURES

10	UCL	3-0	v Alashkert	(Edouard, Forrest, McGregor)
18	UCL	3-0	v Alashkert	(Dembele 2, Forrest)
25	UCL	3-1	v Rosenborg	(Edouard 2, Ntcham)

(Home fixtures in bold)

There was a sign of things to come for Celtic when James Forrest and Callum McGregor added the other goals in Celtic's 3-0 win.

The exact same scoreline was achieved in the second leg for a 6-0 aggregate score over the Armenians with Moussa Dembele scoring the first of the term at Paradise after only seven minutes and adding another from the spot, while Forrest struck again in the 35th minute.

The draw for the next round threw up Rosenborg for the second year running and a magnificent win was engineered at Paradise despite the visitors taking the lead in the 15th minute.

Edouard goals in each half sandwiched an Olivier Ntcham goal right after the break as Celtic powered to a 3-1 win over the Norwegian champions.

REVIEW

TREBLE TREBLE
2016 · 2017
2017 · 2018
2018 · 2019
Celebrating a Trinity of Trebles

THE TREBLE TREBLE CAMPAIGN

SEASON

AUGUST

FIRST up right at the start of the month was Rosenborg away and a well-earned 0-0 draw took the Hoops through by a 3-1 aggregate scoreline.

The Celts then welcomed Livingston on Flag Day at Celtic Park as the SPFL campaign opened with the colours being raised in Paradise for the seventh year in a row. Tom Rogic scored the first goal of the eight-in-a-row bid, while Odsonne Edouard and Olivier Ntcham added before the visitors scored in the last minute of a 3-1 win.

Celtic knew that AEK Athens awaited after Rosenborg in the next Champions League qualifier and although Callum McGregor put the Hoops 1-0 ahead in the 17th minute, they knew it would still be tough against the Greek side. The visitors equalised and won the return tie 2-1 meaning the Celts parachuted into the UEFA Europa League qualifiers.

AUGUST FIXTURES

1	UCL	0-0	v Rosenborg	
4	**SPFL**	**3-1**	**v Livingston**	**(Rogic, Edouard, Ntcham)**
8	**UCL**	**1-1**	**v AEK Athens**	**(McGregor)**
11	SPFL	0-1	v Hearts	
14	UCL	1-2	v AEK Athens	(Sinclair)
18	LC	3-1	v Partick Thistle	(Griffiths, Dembele, Rogic)
23	UEL	1-1	v FK Suduva	(Ntcham)
26	**SPFL**	**1-0**	**v Hamilton Accies**	**(Boyata)**
30	UEL	3-0	v FK Suduva	(Griffiths, McGregor, Ajer)

(Home fixtures in bold)

In between the two Greek games, Celtic lost 1-0 at Tynecastle, but bounced back in their defence of the League Cup with a 3-1 win over Partick Thistle whilst a 4-1 aggregate win over FK Suduva sandwiched a 1-0 SPFL win over Hamilton Accies and took the side into the group stages of the Europa League to finish off the month in style.

THE TOP 3

	P	W	D	L	F	A	GD	Pts
Hearts	3	3	0	0	6	1	5	9
Celtic	3	2	0	1	4	2	2	6
Hibernian	3	1	2	0	5	2	3	4

SEPTEMBER

AMAZINGLY, Celtic never scored more than one goal in any of the September fixtures, but took two important scalps in the league, progressed in the League Cup and, vitally, picked up three crucial points in the Europa League.

The month started off in the best possible way with a 1-0 win over Rangers thanks to an Olivier Ntcham goal in the 62nd minute of a game that Celtic totally dominated.

Those Europa League points came in Group B where Celtic were placed with FC Salzburg, RB Leipzig and, as luck would have it, old foes Rosenborg for the third time in two seasons. And it was against the Norwegian side that Celtic started with a win thanks to a Leigh Griffiths' goal in the 87th minute.

SEPTEMBER FIXTURES

2	SPFL	1-0	v Rangers	(Ntcham)
14	SPFL	0-0	v St Mirren	
20	UEL	1-0	v Rosenborg	(Griffiths)
23	SPFL	1-2	v Kilmarnock	(Griffiths)
26	LC	1-0	v St Johnstone	(Griffiths)
29	SPFL	1-0	v Aberdeen	(Sinclair)

(Home fixtures in bold)

That win came following a 0-0 draw at Championship title-winners, St Mirren and was followed with a 2-1 defeat at Kilmarnock.

Celtic needed a fillip, and that arrived with another 1-0 win in a totally commanding League Cup victory over St Johnstone in Perth thanks to another Griffiths' goal in the 83rd minute, and that was closely followed by a 1-0 win over Aberdeen.

THE TOP 3

	P	W	D	L	F	A	GD	Pts
Hearts	7	6	1	0	13	3	10	19
Hibernian	7	4	2	1	13	6	7	14
Livingston	7	4	2	1	7	4	3	14
Celtic (fifth place)	7	4	1	2	7	4	3	13

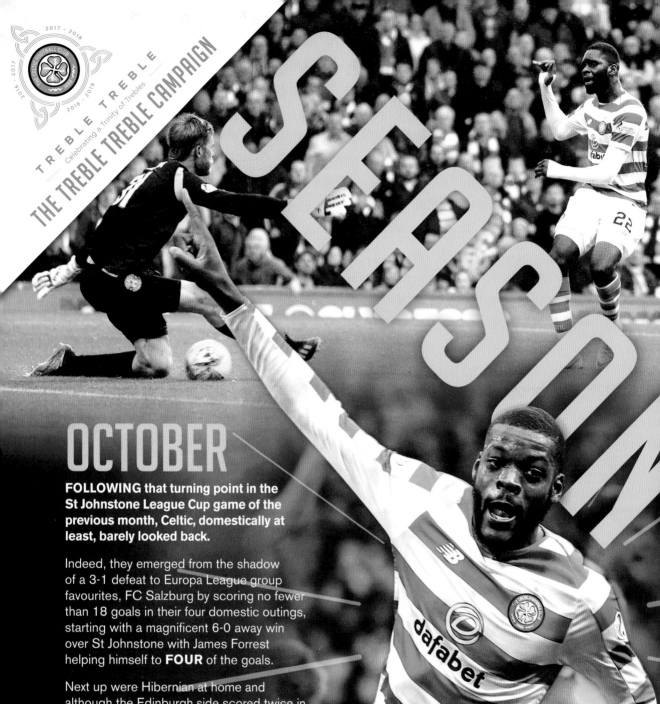

2017 · 2018
2016 · 2017
2018 · 2019

TREBLE TREBLE
Celebrating a Trinity of Trebles

THE TREBLE TREBLE CAMPAIGN

SEASON

OCTOBER

FOLLOWING that turning point in the St Johnstone League Cup game of the previous month, Celtic, domestically at least, barely looked back.

Indeed, they emerged from the shadow of a 3-1 defeat to Europa League group favourites, FC Salzburg by scoring no fewer than 18 goals in their four domestic outings, starting with a magnificent 6-0 away win over St Johnstone with James Forrest helping himself to **FOUR** of the goals.

Next up were Hibernian at home and although the Edinburgh side scored twice in the second half, the win was never in doubt and 4-2 was the final scoreline.

Following losing 2-0 in Leipzig, Celtic were then shunted from Hampden to Murrayfield in the capital to play the other Edinburgh side in the League Cup semi-final with many predicting Hearts would repeat their earlier win in the city.

OCTOBER FIXTURES

4	UEL	1-3	v FC Salzburg	(Edouard)
7	SPFL	6-0	v St Johnstone	(Forrest 4, Edouard, McGregor)
20	**SPFL**	**4-2**	**v Hibernian**	**(Rogic, Ntcham, Edouard 2)**
25	UEL	0-2	v RB Leipzig	
28	LC	3-0	v Hearts	(Sinclair, Forrest, Christie)
31	SPFL	5-0	v Dundee	(Rogic, Sinclair, Forrest, Edouard, Christie)

(Home fixtures in bold)

THE TOP 3

	P	W	D	L	F	A	GD	Pts
Hearts	11	8	2	1	19	7	12	26
Celtic	**10**	**7**	**1**	**2**	**22**	**6**	**16**	**22**
Kilmarnock	11	6	3	2	17	10	7	21

However, second-half substitute, Ryan Christie turned the game by having a hand in two goals and then scoring a cracker himself in a resounding 3-0 win at the home of Scottish rugby.

The goals kept flowing in the final game of the month in a midweek trip to Dens Park where they were spread out in the 5-0 win with Forrest and Christie maintaining their happy knack of finding the net.

TREBLE TREBLE
2017 - 2018
2016 - 2017
2018 - 2019
Celebrating a Trinity of Trebles

THE TREBLE TREBLE CAMPAIGN

SEASON

NOVEMBER

CELTIC started November just as they had finished October a few days earlier – with a resounding 5-0 win. This time the victory was over a side who had defeated the Hoops at the start of the season and, in beating Hearts, the Celts just carried on from their 3-0 League Cup semi-final win over the Edinburgh side.

It was 3-0 by half-time with two Odsonne Edouard goals sandwiching Filip Benkovic's first goal for the club. In the second half, both James Forrest and Ryan Christie, the latter from the spot, kept up their remarkable scoring form.

November, though, was characterised by two excellent European results – one at home and one away. The first coming when Paradise lit up for the visit of RB Leipzig and the lightshow off the park was outshone by the Celts on it with Kieran Tierney and Edouard scoring in a 2-1 win.

THE TOP 3

	P	W	D	L	F	A	GD	Pts
Celtic	13	9	2	2	30	6	24	29
Rangers	13	8	3	2	35	11	24	27
Hearts	14	8	2	4	19	15	4	27

At the end of the month it was a trip to Trondheim that produced the win as Scott Sinclair's goal beat Rosenborg to put the Hoops within one point of guaranteed progress in the UEFA Europa League.

In between those games, a 0-0 draw at Livingston was followed by a 3-0 win at Hamilton Accies in the SPFL.

NOVEMBER FIXTURES

3	SPFL	5-0	v Hearts	(Edouard 2, Benkovic, Forrest, Christie)
8	UEL	2-1	v RB Leipzig	(Tierney, Edouard)
11	SPFL	0-0	v Livingston	
24	SPFL	3-0	v Hamilton Accies	(Christie, Martin og, Griffiths)
29	UEL	1-0	v Rosenborg	(Sinclair)

(Home fixtures in bold)

DECEMBER

CELTIC headed into the final games of 2018 at the top of the league, with the League Cup in the bag, and with UEFA Europa League football to look forward to after Christmas.

The month started with the League Cup being captured once more at Hampden with a 1-0 victory over Aberdeen for a magnificent seventh trophy in a row.

In the league, a 1-1 draw with Motherwell at Fir Park was hardly just reward for the team's domination of the game, but when table-topping Kilmarnock arrived at Celtic Park, a crushing 5-1 defeat was doled out to them from the Hoops.

Celtic knew a point against FC Salzburg would guarantee continental football after Christmas, but despite the 2-1 defeat to a technically-skilled side, a shock 1-1 draw for Rosenborg was hailed from the stands of Paradise in one of those strange scenarios – a magical European night on the back of a defeat. The defeat at Easter Road a few days later wasn't taken quite so lightly, but a sterling 3-0 win over Motherwell midweek put the Celts back on top ahead of meeting Dundee and winning 3-0.

DECEMBER FIXTURES

2	LC	1-0	v Aberdeen	(Christie)
5	SPFL	1-1	v Motherwell	(Christie)
8	**SPFL**	**5-1**	**v Kilmarnock**	**(Forrest 2, Edouard, Lustig, Christie)**
13	**UEL**	**1-2**	**v FC Salzburg**	**(Ntcham)**
16	SPFL	0-2	v Hibernian	
19	**SPFL**	**3-0**	**v Motherwell**	**(Ralston, Sinclair, Johnston)**
22	**SPFL**	**3-0**	**v Dundee**	**(Johnston 2, Benkovic)**
26	SPFL	4-3	v Aberdeen	(Sinclair 3, Edouard)
29	SPFL	0-1	v Rangers	

(Home fixtures in bold)

A thrilling 4-3 win over Aberdeen, the score was just 2-1 with seven minutes left to play, was played out at Pittodrie on Boxing Day. However, a lacklustre display at Ibrox gave Rangers a 1-0 win – their first over Celtic in 13 games. That left both teams locked on 42 points but, ironically, it was Celtic that were to use that game as a springboard to better things in 2019.

THE TOP 3

	P	W	D	L	F	A	GD	Pts
Celtic	**20**	**13**	**3**	**4**	**46**	**14**	**32**	**42**
Rangers	21	12	6	3	43	16	27	42
Kilmarnock	21	12	5	4	32	20	12	41

TREBLE TREBLE
2017 - 2018
2018 - 2019
2016 - 2017
Celebrating a Trinity of Trebles
THE TREBLE TREBLE CAMPAIGN

SEASON

JANUARY

ALTHOUGH the year 2018 finished in deadlock at the top of the table, the month of January ended with the Celts easing away in first place once more and also looking forward to the next round of the Scottish Cup thanks to a 3-0 win over Airdrie.

The surge of success was in no small part due to the warm-weather training camp in Dubai for the winter break while the January transfer window saw Oliver Burke and Timo Weah, both in on loan from West Brom and French side, Paris Saint-Germain respectively, make a pretty immediate mark on the scoring charts.

JANUARY FIXTURES

19	SC	3-0	v Airdrie	(Sinclair 2, Weah)
23	SPFL	4-0	v St Mirren	(Burke 2, Sinclair, Weah)
26	SPFL	3-0	v Hamilton Accies	(McGregor, Christie, Sinclair)
30	SPFL	2-0	v St Johnstone	(McGregor, Christie)

(Home fixtures in bold)

THE TOP 3

	P	W	D	L	F	A	GD	Pts
Celtic	23	16	3	4	55	14	41	51
Rangers	23	13	6	4	47	18	29	45
Kilmarnock	23	13	6	4	34	21	13	45

The window also saw Jeremy Toljan come in on loan at the end of the month from Borussia Dortmund while winger, Marian Shved signed from FC Karpaty, but immediately went back to the Ukrainian outfit on loan for the remainder of the season.

All four January games were at home, all squeezed into an 11-day period and all produced clean sheets for the Celts as they scored 12 goals to no reply while Rangers had kicked-off the New Year with a 2-1 defeat at Kilmarnock.

TREBLE TREBLE
2016 · 2017
2017 · 2018
2018 · 2019
Celebrating a Trinity of Trebles

THE TREBLE TREBLE CAMPAIGN

SEASON

FEBRUARY

WHILE both August and December featured nine games to February's eight, matches at the end of January and start of March ensured that Celtic played TEN games inside a 32-day period.

St Johnstone provided opposition for three of the 10 games while Valencia were played twice and, unfortunately, those games thwarted any hope of further progress in the UEFA Europa League.

Just days after defeating St Johnstone at home, Celtic travelled to Perth and earned a 2-0 win before repeating the same scoreline against Hibernian prior to meeting the Saints once more, this time in the Scottish Cup.

FEBRUARY FIXTURES

3	SPFL	2-0	v St Johnstone	(Forrest, Weah)
6	**SPFL**	**2-0**	**v Hibernian**	**(Christie, Burke)**
10	**SC**	**5-0**	**v St Johnstone**	**(Sinclair 3, Brown, Forrest)**
14	**UEL**	**0-2**	**v Valencia**	
17	SPFL	1-0	v Kilmarnock	(Brown)
21	UEL	0-1	v Valencia	
24	**SPFL**	**4-1**	**v Motherwell**	**(Sinclair, Edouard 2, Burke)**
27	SPFL	2-1	v Hearts	(Forrest, Edouard)

(Home fixtures in bold)

The scoreline in the cup match was a little more emphatic with Scott Sinclair netting a hat-trick in the 5-0 defeat of the Saints, and in Celtic's next domestic outing, Scott Brown not only scored his first goal in two years, but left it until the last minute of the 1-0 win at Kilmarnock.

The Hoops' next game, a 4-1 win over Motherwell that featured the first domestic goal loss of the year – albeit under highly dubious circumstances – also unexpectedly turned out to be Brendan Rodgers' last game in charge.

He departed for Leicester City, but Celtic acted quickly and Neil Lennon was in the dugout for the midweek trip to Tynecastle where a dramatic last-minute goal by Odsonne Edouard delivered a 2-1 win.

THE TOP 3

	P	W	D	L	F	A	GD	Pts
Celtic	28	21	3	4	66	16	50	66
Rangers	28	17	7	4	64	20	44	58
Aberdeen	28	15	5	8	45	33	12	50

2017 - 2018
2016 - 2017
2018 - 2019

TREBLE TREBLE
Celebrating a Trinity of Trebles

THE TREBLE TREBLE CAMPAIGN

SEASON

MARCH

JUST days after leading Celtic to victory over Hearts at Tynecastle, Neil Lennon was back in the capital, this time sending the Celts out to face his former charges, Hibernian, in the Scottish Cup quarter-final.

Ironically, the Easter Road side had a habit of causing problems for Celtic over recent games, but second-half goals from James Forrest and Scott Brown, his third in quick succession sealed the 2-0 win.

THE TOP 3

	P	W	D	L	F	A	GD	Pts
Celtic	31	23	4	4	69	17	52	73
Rangers	31	17	9	5	67	24	43	60
Kilmarnock	31	15	9	7	44	28	16	54

MARCH FIXTURES

2	SC	2-0	v Hibernian	(Forrest, Brown)
9	**SPFL**	**0-0**	**v Aberdeen**	
17	SPFL	1-0	v Dundee	(Edouard)
31	**SPFL**	**2-1**	**v Rangers**	**(Edouard, Forrest)**

(Home fixtures in bold)

The new manager's first game back home in Paradise was less eventful as a well-drilled Aberdeen side held out for a 0-0 draw before a trip to Dundee delivered yet another last-minute winner from Odsonne Edouard.

That left the game on the final day of the month – the first derby meeting since the New Year and a defeat would cut Celtic's lead over Rangers to seven points, while a win would stretch the gap to 13 points.

And 13 it was as strikes from Edouard and Forrest either side of an equaliser from the visitors gave Celtic a 2-1 win on an afternoon of high drama.

2017 - 2018
2016 - 2017
2018 - 2019

TREBLE TREBLE
Celebrating a Trinity of Trebles

THE TREBLE TREBLE CAMPAIGN

SEASON

APRIL

THE month of April was dominated by the passing of two Celtic legends within a week of each other, as Lisbon Lions, Billy McNeill and Stevie Chalmers finally succumbed to their long battles with illness.

The captain of the club's greatest-ever side and the man who scored the winning goal in Lisbon in 1967 joined the Lions who had passed before them.

Sometimes football becomes secondary, but on the day that 60,000 gathered at Celtic Park to pay homage, events on the park brought that day's football and the events of 1967 together in the most apt of ways.

HAIL CESAR

THE TOP 3

	P	W	D	L	F	A	GD	Pts
Celtic	35	25	6	4	72	17	55	81
Rangers	35	21	9	5	78	25	53	72
Aberdeen	35	18	7	10	53	39	14	61

APRIL FIXTURES

3	SPFL	2-0	v St Mirren	(Weah, Christie)
6	**SPFL**	**0-0**	**v Livingston**	
14	SC	3-0	v Aberdeen	(Forrest, Edouard, Rogic)
21	SPFL	0-0	v Hibernian	
27	**SPFL**	**1-0**	**v Kilmarnock**	**(Simunovic)**

(Home fixtures in bold)

Prior to this game, Celtic had won two and drawn two games without losing a goal before the sad news of Billy McNeill's passing.

In a week filled with homage, the biggest tribute was made when the current holder of Cesar's No. 5 shirt, Jozo Simunovic, rose like Celtic's greatest-ever captain did on many occasions and headed home the winner – in the iconic 67th minute.

Just a day later, the man who scored Celtic's most important goal also sadly passed away… they were the men who made Celtic the club it is today.

2017 - 2018
2016 - 2017
2018 - 2019

TREBLE TREBLE
Celebrating a Trinity of Trebles

THE TREBLE TREBLE CAMPAIGN

MAY

AFTER close shaves with the 0-0 draw at Hibernian and the 1-0 home win over Kilmarnock, dependent on results elsewhere as to whether they could be title-clinchers or not, Celtic now had their fate in their own hands.

It did, however, involve a difficult trip to Pittodrie against an Aberdeen side who were more than capable of causing Celtic problems, especially on their own turf where the Hoops clinched a tight 4-3 victory back on Boxing Day.

The home side did, initially, carve out a few glaring opportunities that were passed up for all manner of reasons and Aberdeen paid the price as the first half drew to a close with a wonderful diving header from Mikael Lustig opening the scoring and putting Celtic in the driving seat.

Another header, this time from a corner, saw Jozo Simunovic score for the second successive game to put the Celts 2-0 ahead and eight-in-a-row was just ahead on the horizon.

The win was fully sealed when Odsonne Edouard made it 3-0 and, at the final whistle, there were title-winning celebrations in front of a Celtic crowd for the eighth successive season.

MAY FIXTURES

4	SPFL	3-0	v St Aberdeen	(Lustig, Simunovic, Edouard)
12	SPFL	0-2	v Rangers	
19	**SPFL**	**2-1**	**v Hearts**	**(Johnston 2)**
25	SC	2-1	v Hearts	(Edouard 2)

(Home fixtures in bold)

A lacklustre display at Ibrox the following week left just two games against Hearts – on Trophy Day and the Scottish Cup final.

Both finished 2-1 for the Hoops to see that the club finished both competitions on a high and, more importantly, Edouard's two goals at Hampden ensured that Celtic came from behind to not only lift the Scottish Cup, but also seal the seemingly unattainable Treble Treble.

REVIEW

THE TOP 3

	P	W	D	L	F	A	GD	Pts
Celtic	38	27	6	5	77	20	57	87
Rangers	38	23	9	6	82	27	55	78
Kilmarnock	38	19	10	9	50	31	19	67

WHAT CELTIC MEANS TO ME...
PART ONE

WE all want to play for Celtic and we all know what the Hoops mean to us. But what does Celtic mean to the players who actually wear the Hoops?

We talked to some of your heroes to find out exactly what Celtic means to them.

SCOTT BROWN

When I first signed, I loved the fact that the fans always expected you to win. I enjoy winning, I enjoy picking up trophies, and that's one of the reasons I came to Celtic – to win games, to be the best in Scotland, and we've done that over a number of years. That's why I'm still here, and why I'm still enjoying my football and playing with a smile on my face.

JONNY HAYES

Being Irish, I've always known how big the club is. I have a lot of friends and family who are big Celtic fans and it's amazing to see how far-reaching Celtic's support is.

KRISTOFFER AJER

To play in front of 60,000 people and walk out on to the pitch at Celtic Park and hear *You'll Never Walk Alone* is something really special. Those moments are unlike anything else in life and are something that will stay with me forever.

SCOTT BAIN

It's unbelievable. You don't realise the size of the club until you're here and how it's people's lives, it takes over a whole aspect of their life. It's a culture, and to be a part of that, to be able to play for a club the size of Celtic is amazing.

PARADISE PROFILES

SCOTT BROWN

JAMES FORREST

CRAIG GORDON

TOM ROGIC

SCOTT SINCLAIR

LEIGH GRIFFITHS

CALLUM McGREGOR

NIR BITTON

JOZO SIMUNOVIC

EBOUE KOUASSI

JONNY HAYES

RYAN CHRISTIE

KRISTOFFER AJER

OLIVIER NTCHAM

CALVIN MILLER

MIKEY JOHNSTON

ODSONNE EDOUARD

JACK HENDRY

SCOTT BAIN

LEWIS MORGAN

DANNY ARZANI

VAKOUN ISSOUF BAYO

MARIAN SHVED

CONOR HAZARD

KARAMOKO DEMBELE

ARMSTRONG OKO-FLEX

BOLI BOLINGOLI-MBOMBO

CHRISTOPHER JULLIEN

LUCA CONNELL

HATEM ABD ELHAMED

FRASER FORSTER

MORITZ BAUER

GREG TAYLOR

MOHAMED ELYOUNOUSSI

SCOTT BROWN

Position: Midfielder
Squad Number: 8
D.O.B: 25/06/85
Born: Dunfermline, Scotland
Height: 5'10"
Signed: 29/05/07
Debut: v Kilmarnock (h) 0-0, (SPL) 05/08/07
Previous Clubs: Hibernian

JAMES FORREST

Position: Winger
Squad Number: 49
D.O.B: 07/07/91
Born: Prestwick, Scotland
Height: 5'9"
Signed: 01/07/09
Debut: v Motherwell (h) 4-0, (SPL) 01/05/10
Previous Clubs: Celtic Youth

CRAIG GORDON

Position: Goalkeeper
Squad Number: 1
D.O.B: 31/12/82
Born: Edinburgh, Scotland
Height: 6'4"
Signed: 03/07/14
Debut: v St Johnstone (a) 3-0, (SPFL) 13/08/14
Previous Clubs: Sunderland, Hearts, Cowdenbeath (loan)

TOM ROGIC

Position: Midfielder
Squad Number: 18
D.O.B: 16/12/92
Born: Griffith, Australia
Height: 6'2"
Signed: 09/01/13
Debut: v Inverness Caley Thistle (a) 3-1, (SPL) 09/02/13
Previous Clubs: Central Coast Mariners, Belconnen
United, ANU FC

SCOTT SINCLAIR

Position: Midfielder **Squad Number:** 11
D.O.B: 25/03/89 **Born:** Bath, England
Height: 5' 10" **Signed:** 07/08/16
Debut: v Hearts (a) 2-1, (SPFL) 07/08/16
Previous Clubs: Aston Villa, Aston Villa (loan), West Bromwich Albion (loan), Manchester City, Swansea City, Wigan Athletic (loan), Birmingham City (loan), Crystal Palace (loan), Charlton Athletic (loan), Queens Park Rangers (loan), Plymouth Argyle (loan), Chelsea, Bristol Rovers

LEIGH GRIFFITHS

Position: Striker
Squad Number: 9
D.O.B: 20/08/90
Born: Edinburgh, Scotland
Height: 5'9"
Signed: 31/01/14
Debut: v Aberdeen (a) 1-2, (SPFL) 08/02/14
Previous Clubs: Wolverhampton Wanderers, Hibernian (loan), Dundee, Livingston

CALLUM McGREGOR

Position: Midfielder
Squad Number: 42
D.O.B: 14/06/93
Born: Glasgow, Scotland
Height: 5'10"
Debut: v KR Reykjavik (a) 1-0, (UCL) 15/07/14
Previous Clubs: Notts County (loan)

NIR BITTON

Position: Midfielder
Squad Number: 6
D.O.B: 30/10/91
Born: Ashdod, Israel
Height: 6'5"
Signed: 30/08/13
Debut: v AC Milan (a) 0-2, (UCL) 18/09/13
Previous Clubs: FC Ashdod

JOZO SIMUNOVIC

Position: Defender
Squad Number: 5
D.O.B: 04/08/94
Born: Zagreb, Croatia
Height: 6'3''
Signed: 02/09/15
Debut: v Ajax (a) 2-2, (UEL) 17/09/15
Previous Clubs: Dinamo Zagreb

EBOUE KOUASSI

Position: Midfielder
Squad Number: 88
D.O.B: 13/12/97
Born: Abidjan, Ivory Coast
Height: 6' 1"
Signed: 12/01/17
Debut: v St Mirren (h) 4-1, (Scottish Cup) 05/03/17
Previous Clubs: Krasnodar, Shirak

JONNY HAYES

Position: Midfielder
Squad Number: 15
D.O.B: 09/07/87
Born: Dublin, Ireland
Height: 5' 6"
Signed: 19/07/17
Debut: v Linfield (a) 2-0, (UCL) 14/08/17
Previous Clubs: Aberdeen, Inverness Caley Thistle, Cheltenham
Town (loan), Northampton Town (loan), Leicester City, Milton
Keynes Dons (loan), Forest Green Rovers (loan), Reading

RYAN CHRISTIE

Position: Midfielder
Squad Number: 17
D.O.B: 22/02/95
Born: Inverness, Scotland
Height: 5'10''
Signed: 01/09/15
Debut: v St Johnstone (h) 3-1, (SPFL) 23/01/16
Previous Clubs: Inverness Caledonian Thistle,
Aberdeen (loan)

KRISTOFFER AJER

Position: Midfielder
Squad Number: 35
D.O.B: 17/04/98
Born: Raelingen, Norway
Height: 5' 9"
Signed: 17/02/16
Debut: v Lincoln Red Imps (h) 3-0, (UCL) 20/07/16
Previous Clubs: IK Start, Kilmarnock (loan)

OLIVIER NTCHAM

Position: Midfielder
Squad Number: 21
D.O.B: 09/02/96
Born: Longjumeau, France
Height: 5' 9"
Signed: 12/07/17
Debut: v Linfield (h) 4-0, (UCL) 19/08/17
Previous Clubs: Genoa (loan), Manchester City

CALVIN MILLER

Position: Defender
Squad Number: 59
D.O.B: 09/01/98
Born: Glasgow, Scotland
Height: 5' 11"
Debut: v Partick Thistle (h) 1-0, (SPFL) 20/12/16
Previous Clubs: Dundee (loan), Ayr United (loan)

MIKEY JOHNSTON

Position: Striker
Squad Number: 73
D.O.B: 19/04/99
Born: Glasgow, Scotland
Height: 5' 10"
Debut: v St Johnstone (h) 4-1, (SPFL) 06/05/17
Previous Clubs: Celtic Youth

ODSONNE EDOUARD

Position: Striker
Squad Number: 22
D.O.B: 16/01/98
Born: Kourou, French Guiana
Height: 6'1"
Signed: 31/08/17
Debut: v Hamilton Accies (a) 4-1, (SPFL) 08/09/18
Previous Clubs: Toulouse (loan), Paris Saint-Germain

JACK HENDRY

Position: Defender
Squad Number: 4
D.O.B: 07/05/95
Born: Glasgow, Scotland
Height: 6'2"
Signed: 31/01/18
Debut: v Kilmarnock (a) 0-1, (SPFL) 03/02/18
Previous Clubs: Dundee, Milton Keynes Dons (loan), Shrewsbury Town (loan), Wigan Athletic, Partick Thistle, Celtic Youth

SCOTT BAIN

Position: Goalkeeper
Squad Number: 29
D.O.B: 22/11/91
Born: Edinburgh, Scotland
Height: 6'0"
Signed: 31/01/18
Debut: v Rangers (a) 3-2, (SPFL) 11/03/18
Previous Clubs: Hibernian (loan), Dundee, Alloa Athletic, Elgin City (loan), Aberdeen

LEWIS MORGAN

Position: Midfielder
Squad Number: 16
D.O.B: 30/09/96
Born: Greenock, Scotland
Height: 5'8"
Signed: 05/01/18
Debut: v Alashkert (a) 3-0, (UCL) 10/07/18
Previous Clubs: St Mirren, Sunderland (loan)

DANNY ARZANI

Position: Midfielder
Squad Number: 14
D.O.B: 04/01/99
Born: Khorramabad, Iran
Height: 5'7"
Signed: 17/08/18
Debut: v Dundee (a) 5-0, (SPFL) 31/10/18
Previous Clubs: Manchester City, Melbourne City

VAKOUN ISSOUF BAYO

Position: Striker
Squad Number: 10
D.O.B: 10/01/97
Born: Daloa, Ivory Coast
Height: 6'0"
Signed: 08/01/18
Debut: v Kilmarnock (a) 0-1, (SPFL) 17/02/19
Previous Clubs: Dunajska Streda, Etoile du Sahel

MARIAN SHVED

Position: Midfielder
Squad Number: 20
D.O.B: 16/07/97
Born: Mykolaiv, Ukraine
Height: 5'7"
Signed: 30/01/19
Debut: v Nomme Kalju (a) 2-0, (UCL) 30/07/19
Previous Clubs: Karpaty Lviv, Sevilla

CONOR HAZARD

Position: Goalkeeper
Squad Number: 65
D.O.B: 05/03/98
Born: Downpatrick, Ireland
Height: 6' 5"
Signed: 20/05/14
Debut: n/a
Previous Clubs: Celtic Youth

KARAMOKO DEMBELE

Position: Midfielder
Squad Number: 77
D.O.B: 22/02/03
Born: London, England
Height: 5'3"
Debut: v Hearts (h) 2-1, (SPFL) 19/5/19
Previous Clubs: Celtic Youth

ARMSTRONG OKO-FLEX

Position: Midfielder
Squad Number: 48
D.O.B: 02/03/02
Born: Dublin, Ireland
Height: 6'0"
Signed: 31/08/18
Debut: n/a
Previous Clubs: Arsenal Youth

BOLI BOLINGOLI-MBOMBO

Position: Defender
Squad Number: 23
D.O.B: 01/07/95
Born: Antwerp, Belgium
Height: 5'11"
Signed: 03/07/19
Debut: v FK Sarajevo (a) 3-1, (UCL) 9/07/19
Previous Clubs: Rapid Vienna, Sint-Truidense (loan),
Club Brugge

CHRISTOPHER JULLIEN

Position: Defender
Squad Number: 2
D.O.B: 22/03/93
Born: Lagny-sur-Marne, France
Height: 6'5"
Signed: 28/06/19
Debut: v Nomme Kalju (a) 2-0, (UCL) 30/07/19
Previous Clubs: Toulouse, Dijon (loan), SC Freiburg,
Auxerre

LUCA CONNELL

Position: Midfielder
Squad Number: 28
D.O.B: 20/04/01
Born: Liverpool, England
Height: 5'10"
Signed: 29/06/19
Debut: n/a
Previous Clubs: Bolton Wanderers

HATEM ABD ELHAMED

Position: Defender
Squad Number: 33
D.O.B: 18/03/91
Born: Kafr Manda, Israel
Height: 6'1"
Signed: 24/07/19
Debut: v St Johnstone (h) 7-0, (SFPL) 03/08/19
Previous Clubs: Hapoel Be'er Sheva, FC Ashdod (loan), Gent, Dinamo Bucharest (loan), FC Ashdod, Charleroi (loan), Maccabi Tel Aviv

FRASER FORSTER

Position: Goalkeeper
Squad Number: 67
D.O.B: 17/03/88
Born: Hexham, England
Height: 6'7"
Signed: 01/08/10 and 22/08/19
Debut: v Hearts (h) 3-1 (SPFL) 25/08/19
Previous Clubs: Southampton, Celtic, Celtic (loan), Norwich City (loan), Bristol Rovers (loan), Stockport County (loan), Newcastle United.

MORITZ BAUER

Position: Defender
Squad Number: 13
D.O.B: 25/01/92
Born: Winterthur, Switzerland
Height: 5'11"
Signed: 28/08/19
Debut: v Rangers (a) 2-0, (SPFL) 01/09/19
Previous Clubs: Stoke City, Rubin Kazan, Grasshopper Club Zurich, FC Winterthur

GREG TAYLOR

Position: Defender
Squad Number: 3
D.O.B: 05/11/97
Born: Greenock, Scotland
Height: 5'8"
Signed: 02/09/19
Debut: n/a
Previous Clubs: Kilmarnock

MOHAMED ELYOUNOUSSI

Position: Forward
Squad Number: 27
D.O.B: 04/08/94
Born: Al Hoceima, Morocco
Height: 5'10"
Signed: 30/08/19
Debut: n/a
Previous Clubs: Southampton, Basel, Molde, Sarpsborg 08

HOME AND AWAY...
PART TWO

HOME is where the heart is, and we all know what Paradise means to us as Celtic's home ground. What about the players' home towns, though – or their favourite holiday destinations?

We spoke to a few more of the players to find out where they were brought up and where they go during the close season.

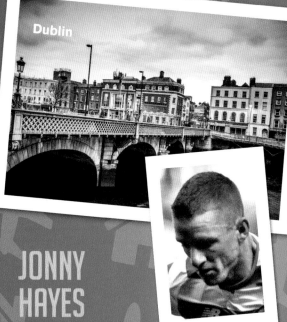

Dublin

Dubai

JONNY HAYES

Home
I come from a place called Ballyfermot in Dublin. I was born there and all my family are from there. I lived there until I was 15-years-old and then I moved to Reading.

Away
I have two young kids now so I normally like to go somewhere reasonably close to home. We usually go over to Portugal for a few weeks every year. My favourite place to go to is probably Dubai.

SCOTT BROWN

Home
Hill of Beath. Lovely place. It's got a hill, a field and cows!

Away
I like to go to Dubai. It's quiet, it's chilled out, nobody really knows you and it's a great place to visit with the family.

Portugal

Marbella

Dalkeith

KRISTOFFER AJER

Home
I'm from Lillestrom in Norway. It's a small city but it was a lovely place to grow up in.

Away
Santorini is a really beautiful place. It's a Greek Island. I haven't been there yet but I would love to go. In terms of places I've been, I would say Rome.

SCOTT BAIN

Home
I'm from a little town outside of Edinburgh called Dalkeith. There's not really much there, just a high street and other small surrounding towns, so it's quite quiet. It's about 15 minutes from Edinburgh which isn't a bad location to be in, being close to the city and still quiet.

Away
I was in Marbella recently with Jack Hendry, getting some sun. I bumped into "Broony" there who was on a golf holiday. Marbella was lovely, though, a great place.

Rome

Lillestrom

SPOT THE DIFFERENCE

THERE are 10 differences between these two photographs. The first one has been circled, but can you spot the rest?

Answers on pages 62/63

MIX 'N' MATCH

See if you can match up the correct Celtic facts from the Treble Treble squad.

1. Kristoffer Ajer signed from this side.

2. He scored twice in the Scottish Cup final.

3. Jozo Simunovic plays for this country.

4. Jonny Hayes started with this side.

5. This player scored the winner in the League Cup final.

6. Leigh Griffiths has caps for this country.

7. This player made the most appearances last season.

8. Celtic played a domestic game here for the first time.

9. Debut Bhoy who won a place on the Scottish Cup final bench.

10. The Glasgow ground Celtic played at only once last season.

MURRAYFIELD

IK START

CROATIA

KARAMOKO DEMBELE

ODSONNE EDOUARD

SCOTLAND

READING

RYAN CHRISTIE

CALLUM McGREGOR

FIRHILL

Find out if you're right on pages 62/63

LEAGUE CUP WIN No.18
THE TREBLE TREBLE STORY PART ONE

AS soon as the final whistle blew at Hampden on Sunday, December 2, 2018, Celtic knew the Treble Treble was very much on – or at least the players and fans knew they were a third of the way to a third successive clean sweep of Scottish trophies.

Just one slip in any cup game could see all thoughts of a treble, never mind the Treble Treble consigned to the bin, but, once more, this Celtic side stood firm and turned it on exactly when it mattered – in another cup final.

If the truth be known, though, such was the expectation surrounding a prospective Treble Treble and highly-motivated opposition, every cup game was a final for Celtic.

As in the 2016/17 Invincible Treble when Celtic lifted their 100th trophy, Aberdeen represented

the final hurdle for Celtic in the League Cup, and this time it was Ryan Christie who was goal hero on the day when he pounced deep into time added on in the first half.

Indeed, Celtic had much to thank Christie for in the semi-final against Hearts at Murrayfield in the capital. After coming on as a substitute, he took centre-stage by winning the penalty that was tucked away by Scott Sinclair, and set up James Forrest for his strike, as well as scoring a screamer of a goal himself in a 3-0 win at the home of Scottish Rugby.

Celtic earlier kicked off their defence of the trophy with a 3-1 win over Partick Thistle before beating St Johnstone 1-0 ahead of the semi-final with Hearts that paved the way for the showdown with the Dons.

In the fourth minute of time added on before the half-time whistle, Dedryck Boyata found Christie in the final third. The midfielder controlled the ball superbly on his left before firing a shot at goal with his right foot that was saved by Joe Lewis. However, Christie fired the rebound into the net.

At the end of the next 45 minutes, the final whistle sparked great scenes of green-and-white celebrations on the pitch and in the stands as the Hoops celebrated another silverware success and the first vital step towards the historic Treble Treble.

CHAMPIONSHIP WIN No.50
THE TREBLE TREBLE STORY
PART TWO

CELTIC took a step closer to the possible Treble Treble by lifting their eighth title in a row and, amid all the deserved celebration, it went almost unnoticed that this indeed was another milestone for the Hoops – it was the club's 50th title win.

The title was clinched three games from the end of the campaign in a stylish 3-0 win over Aberdeen at Pittodrie as the Celts showed their mettle in what could have been a potentially very difficult 90 minutes against the home side.

Goals from Mikael Lustig, Jozo Simunovic and Odsonne Edouard illustrated Celtic's will to win and ensured that the Hoops' next home game would be Trophy Day at Celtic Park for the eighth consecutive season.

On the big day, two goals from teenager, Mikey Johnston sealed the 2-1 win that saw Celtic finish nine points ahead of Rangers, and also paved the way for a winning celebration as club legend, Paul McStay delivered the SPFL trophy to the hallowed turf.

Now, Celtic were just 90 minutes away from an unprecedented Treble Treble.

Ladbrokes PREMIERSHIP

2018/19 WINNERS

CELTIC FOOTBALL CLUB

SCOTTISH CUP WIN No.39
THE TREBLE TREBLE STORY PART THREE

FOR the first time ever, despite the odd close call, Celtic lifted the Scottish Cup for a third successive season, and, in turn, completed the Treble Treble – the Trinity of Trebles.

The most successful side in Scottish Cup history lifted the world's oldest football trophy for the 39th time on May 25, 2019, coming back from 1-0 down to win 2-1, just as the Lisbon Lions had done in the European Cup final on the same date 52 years earlier on May 25, 1967.

The Scottish Cup final date was apt, as the Celts paid tribute to the two Lions who had recently passed away – Billy McNeill and Stevie Chalmers

– by wearing warm-up tracksuit tops emblazoned with the names of the Celtic legends and wearing both No.5 and No.9 on their shorts.

And the team came up with the goods to pay a fitting tribute to the man who lifted the European Cup and the man who scored the goal that won it, as they once more showed the resilience that had delivered the previous eight successive domestic trophies.

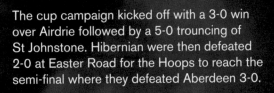

The cup campaign kicked off with a 3-0 win over Airdrie followed by a 5-0 trouncing of St Johnstone. Hibernian were then defeated 2-0 at Easter Road for the Hoops to reach the semi-final where they defeated Aberdeen 3-0.

That left Hearts in the final standing between Celtic and the Treble Treble, and the Edinburgh side seemed to stick a spanner in the works when they took the lead seven minutes after the break.

However, Odsonne Edouard equalised from the spot after he was brought down in the box and, just eight minutes from the end, the Frenchman latched on to a clearing header from Mikael Lustig and expertly placed the ball behind the keeper – Celtic had won nine consecutive trophies, and the Treble Treble was a reality.

TREBLE TREBLE
Celebrating a trinity of Trebles

COLOURING-IN

TIME to get out the crayons, paintbrush or coloured marker pens and bring this picture to life with glorious Celticolour. But who is it and where is he?

Solution on pages 62/63

TREBLE TREBLE SEASON QUIZ

1. Which player scored the first domestic goal of the Treble Treble campaign?
2. Celtic played only one home game in six October matches – who was it against?
3. Who scored both goals in Celtic's Trophy Day win over Hearts?
4. Who were the only three Celts to score in all three domestic competitions?
5. Which three Celts totalled just one substitute appearance each during the season?
6. Scott Martin scored an own goal for Celtic, which team was he playing for?
7. Which Celt reached 500 Celtic appearances during the season?
8. Who was Celtic's top scorer?
9. What was Neil Lennon's first game back in charge of the team?
10. Which defender scored in two successive league games?

Answers on pages 62/63

FROM LENNOXTOWN TO PARADISE

A **CELTIC** player about to make his debut has to make his way from the Lennoxtown Training Complex to Celtic Park for a press conference.

Can you help him get there?

LENNOXTOWN

CELTIC PARK

Find out how he got there on pages 62/63

THE EIGHT-IN-A-ROW BHOYS

HOOPS captain Scott Brown, along with Mikael Lustig and James Forrest are the trio of Celts who have played in every one of the eight-in-a-row championships.

So much so, that end-of-season Trophy Day celebrations have become a way of life for the three Celts who have each made massive contributions to the success of the team over the past eight league campaigns.

The skipper has appeared in 228 of the 304 Celtic games played throughout the run that has seen the Hoops dominate the game throughout the decade.

The Swedish defender, who has since departed for Gent in Belgium, arrived just in time to join in at the start of the run and his goal celebrations, whether he scored the goal or not, have become the stuff of legend.

James Forrest said goodbye to his teenage years just weeks before the first campaign began and is now an established Scotland internationalist with a raft of individual honours picked up during last season.

The trio have joined the ranks of Billy McNeill, Bobby Murdoch, Jimmy Johnstone and Bobby Lennox who all played in each of Celtic's first eight-in-a-row under the great Jock Stein.

PLAYER	A	S	G
SCOTT BROWN	220	8	15
JAMES FORREST	151	44	44
MIKAEL LUSTIG	145	16	13
TOTAL	517	68	72

WHAT CELTIC MEANS TO ME...
PART TWO

WE all want to play for Celtic and we all know what the Hoops mean to us. But what does Celtic mean to the players who actually wear the Hoops?

Here, we talk to some more of your heroes to find out exactly what Celtic means to them.

JOZO SIMUNOVIC

All the words I have about Celtic are overwhelmingly positive. All the people I have met at the club, from the staff, the players, the coaches and the fans, have been amazing. It means a lot to us as players and it motivates us to always want to give more and more. I'm never happy with what I've accomplished because that's in the past and I always try to focus on the present.

CRAIG GORDON

It means a lot to me. To be in a successful team is great and to be in a team that has accomplished what we have is really special. The support is amazing and years down the line I think we'll realise how special this time was. You don't get this at every club and that's what makes it special to me.

RYAN CHRISTIE

It's brilliant to play for the club. When I was younger, I was a Celtic fan, along with my whole family, so to be in the position I am now is quite surreal. I have to remind myself of that sometimes – of how important a feeling it should be to play for this club, and I think that's all the motivation you need to break into a squad, which is good.

MIKEY JOHNSTON

It's different for some people as they are obviously not supporters, but this is my local club. It's five or 10 minutes down the road from me, so it's mad to play for the team that you've always supported. I watched them when I was younger and I watched Scott Brown on the telly and now I'm in a dressing room with him and being on the park with them is weird. I don't really think about pinching myself when I'm on the park, though. I just get on with it as I'm there for a reason because I've worked hard to get there, so you just have to believe in your own ability.

THE TREBLE TREBLE NUMBERS' GAME

A look at just some of the historical figures from Celtic's domination of the past three seasons

WINNING MENTALITY

112 VICTORIES

339 GOALS

CELTIC WON 79% OF ALL GAMES AND HAD 67 GAMES UNDEFEATED IN PARADISE

NET PROPHET

52 GOALS FOR SCOTT SINCLAIR WHO FINISHED AS TREBLE TREBLE TOP SCORER

JEEPERS KEEPERS

86 CLEAN SHEETS FOR CRAIG GORDON, SCOTT BAIN AND DORUS DE VRIES

WENT OVER 60% OF MATCHES WITHOUT CONCEDING A GOAL

MEDAL DETECTOR

19 MEDALS FOR SCOTT BROWN TO EQUAL JIMMY JOHNSTONE'S TROPHY HAUL AND BECOME JOINT THIRD IN CELTIC'S ALL-TIME LIST

GLOBAL APPEAL

21 DIFFERENT NATIONALITIES PLAYED FOR CELTIC IN THE TREBLE TREBLE FROM THE 51 PLAYERS USED

CUP KINGS

27

WINS IN A ROW WITH

MAGICAL AND WONDERFUL

127 APPEARANCES FOR SCOTT SINCLAIR, WHILE CALLUM McGREGOR PLAYED IN 125 GAMES AND SCOTT BROWN FEATURED IN 122

83

GOALS AND

23

CLEAN SHEETS

9

HAT-TRICK HEROES

NINE HAT-TRICKS WERE SCORED THROUGHOUT THE TREBLE TREBLE WITH FOUR DIFFERENT PLAYERS TAKING THE MATCH BALL HOME – SCOTT SINCLAIR (3), MOUSSA DEMBELE (3), JAMES FORREST (2) AND ODSONNE EDOUARD (1)

UNBEATABLE

69 GAMES UNDEFEATED AND DURING THE RUN, THE INVINCIBLES RECORDED 27 STRAIGHT WINS

ANSWERS

PAGE 46: SPOT THE DIFFERENCE

PAGE 47: MIX 'N' MATCH

Here are the answers from the Treble Treble squad mix-up teaser.

1. Kristoffer Ajer signed from this side _____ IK Start

2. He scored twice in the Scottish Cup final _____ Odsonne Edouard

3. Jozo Simunovic plays for this country _____ Croatia

4. Jonny Hayes started with this side _____ Reading

5. This player scored the winner in the League Cup final _____ Ryan Christie

6. Leigh Griffiths has caps for this country _____ Scotland

7. This player made the most appearances last season _____ Callum McGregor

8. Celtic played a domestic game here for the first time _____ Murrayfield

9. Debut Bhoy who won a place on the Scottish Cup final bench _____ Karamoko Dembele

10. The Glasgow ground Celtic played at only once last season _____ Firhill